THE
SECRET'S OF LIFE

JASMINE BURDINE

PROMINENT
BOOKS
EDGE

5830 E 2nd St, Ste 7000 #9983
Casper, WY 82609
USA

Contents

Chapter 1
SORROWS

Chapter 2
LOVE GAIN & LOVE LOST

Chapter 3
TRAP

Chapter 1

SORROWS

Ruff Neck

She's ruff neck
Even though she's gorgeous
She's very defiant in everything
she does
Intellectual she stays compelling
Oh how marvelous she can be
Given the opportunities that's
presented from every door
Even though she had a hard life
no doubt
She always stayed composed
Like she was implanting an
operation
Like she was playing a game of
chess with no remorse
Her mindset was her freedom and
her words are her armor
She held herself up so high that no
man could touch her
It's not like she didn't want them to
It's the fact she didn't know how to
In all actuality she really had problems

Just going by what her stepdad did
to her
Sexually assaulting her verbally
abusing her
Even though that's not what
screwed up her conscience
It's the fact that her mom knew
about it and try to deny it
With all the drama and the
domestic violence
Baby girl stayed silent
She was a fighter
Whether they knew it or not
She was going to be a survivor
So, she kept her head up high
And with God's help she was able to
reach the sky
Still until this day people would
never know
Why she came off harsh or why she
stayed to herself

Why she barley said any words like
　　nothing matter to her
It's just they didn't know
She was living a living hell
They didn't know her story
Because she never tells

Sorry

Sorry if I wasn't the best dad,
   the best dad I could've been
   That I couldn't really support
   you and your mom the way I
   really wanted too
I was still young trying to figure out
   who I really am
Since I was drinking a hell of a lot
   and not really giving a damn
I was like, "fuck being a dad"
I really don't know how to raise a
   boy into a man
But for you I'll try
For you I'd give more than I ever can
Because my dad wasn't shit
I didn't care if he lives or die
That man wasn't ever there in my life
But for you I wanted
   something better
Even if I didn't know how to be

See, you was my king
Every time I hold you
I can feel myself getting all
   wrapped up inside
Like I was proud to be a dad but
   mad at the same time
When I look at you
I question why I ever hated you
Why I ever wished you weren't born
It wasn't your fault
Your mom chose not to get
   that abortion
Now I'm glad she didn't
Now I feel like I could make
   a difference
Starting with me and you I can
   change this cycle of a dead-
   beat dad and I thank you
   for that

Living In Pain

She has no name; She covers
her pain
with fake laughter and joy
She tries to deny the fact she ever
had dreams
That she ever once believed that
there's possibilities of her
finding real joy
In her own little messed up world
She can't seem to forget the scars
That was marked upon her as a
young child
Trying to hide them from her mom
so she wouldn't get locked in
the basement most of the time
She'll chain her up as if she was
a dog
So, she couldn't run away even if
she wanted too
Had her begging just to go back to
her room
Just to play with her little piece of
crap dolls

Just so she could only pretend she
was once just a normal little
girl again
Her mother always felt like she
was a burden on her physically
and mentally
So, she never really had love for her
The fact she ends up looking like
her dad made her hate her
own daughter
That was the only reason why she
had her in the first place
But he left her after a few days
she was boring for a whole
another woman
The fact that her daughter was
such a beautiful little girl made
her upset most of the time only
because she looks way better
than her mom
So, she stayed doing her best to
leave her alone in the house

With different kind of men, she'll
    sleep with now and then
Some was kind; I'll admit
Then some was worse than her mom
The one's she remembers the most
    are those who did late night visits
    to her room
Pretending to read her a bedtime
    story so her mom wouldn't know
How many times she had cried she
    lost count
Just as she did when it came to how
    many men of her mom had given
    her those special late-night visit
But nobody knows of this little girl
Who hid from her mom so she
    wouldn't get abused most of
    the time
Who cried herself to sleep
    most nights

Who ran away from home through
    her mind
Because that was a place where she
    could escape the harsh reality,
    she was living
If you saw today
She'll come off as sweet and kind
Loud and outspoken only when it
    comes to her mind
But yet she'll appear quite like she's
    not really here
Like she's fighting herself to come
    back to reality
Yet she's stuck in a trance where she
    can't be found
Where nobody knows who she is
Therefore she doesn't exist
Only as a lost little girl and that's it

The Lost Boy

He looked so innocent doing
this shit
That no one would believe he
was doing this
Taking niggas lives like he was
snatchin' up toys at a toy store
He was just a boy only eleven
years old
But he looks up to the wrong men
Who took good care of him
They washed him, they clothed him
Teaching him their way on how to
be a man
Turning him into a natural
born killer
They finally got inside of his head
Now he's like a deadly bomb
It never takes him that much
to make him go off with no
stop signs
People say you can even hear
the ticking of death on his
clock ticking

When he walks by or even when he's
gunning for you
If you're his target believe me you
won't see him
He hides in the dark with a mask
over his face with gloves on
Nothing but black on
Ready to hunt like a lion does when
it's hungry
He stayed strap no matter who
he trusts
When you're dying, he likes to take
off his mask to show you who
he really is
They'll be like, "Damn, you're just a
little boy."
He would be like, no more
Then he'll let another round go off
killing them fast
Before they start choking on their
own blood
He was the best hitman, as no one
knew who he was

But once they find out
You could already guess what happened
Yes, he was eleven years old, and as
    the story goes
Don't move too fast, because you will
    get caught up, just like this little
    boy once did

Thirteen

Thirteen looking like she's in her early twenties
Momma isn't there; she's always out working
Daddy was never there; she never met him in person
Nobody sees what's actually happening
She's thirteen messing around with grow men
Lying about her age so they aren't questioning
She loves feeling wanted
She also loves the attention
She loves the things she receive
That's why she isn't stopping
Her friend is with it
That's where she learned it
Her friend showed her how to really do it
She's thirteen and not making good decisions

She's thirteen and I bet you won't be able to see it
Her body is nicely shaped so every guy wants a piece of it
Got thick hips and thighs so someone is always checking her
Her breast and butt got guys doing a double-take
No matter what sexy, tight clothes she wears to show off her figure
No matter how much makeup she puts on,
I can still see the little girl who is hidden
That she's fighting not to be
She is thirteen and looking for love in all the wrong places
She's thirteen and her mom needs to come gets her
So, none of these grown men doesn't snatch her

I cannot tell you how many of these
girls go missing
I can't tell you how many of these
girls end up in prostitution
Running toward the wrong guy; now
there's no solution
I can't tell you how many got so
caught up that now they're no
longer living
Be careful, thirteen; not everybody is
your friend
Be careful at thirteen you should
start being a kid again

He Stops

He stops coming around for me
Now he's actin' like he
doesn't even know me
He just stares at me without saying
one word to me
He doesn't even smile for me
I can't even make him laugh he just
look sad
He was my best friend until his
brother pass
Now he's not even here; his mind
stays elsewhere
No matter how much I try he just
won't open up to me
In his eyes everything is dark and
cold with mold
He really thinks he's alone
He thinks no one can feel his pain
or understand his reason
He stops showing up to class
He used to come late but he
always came

Now he doesn't even bother
to come
It's like he doesn't even care
anymore
It's like no one can comfort him
It's like he wants to be left alone
& depressed
He's starting to believe God was
never there for him
If his brother was still here; I know
he would be feeling differently
Since he been praying for so long
His brother still got taken away
He lost faith in everything
Everything is a joke, a game
He's playing along not questioning
one word anymore
It really hurts seeing him every time
when he walks by
It's like seeing a ghost there's
no emotions
You could tell his soul is broken

He doesn't even know after the
    rain storm
There's always a sunny day that
    comes right after
He's slowly going away
When he goes to his brother grave
He automatically breaks down
He let's all his feelings out
Saying why you had to go and leave
    me all alone
You know I can't do nothing right
    when your gone
I miss you while his eyes are full
    of tears
Even though I can see him
Some how I don't say a word
Instead I just walk right up towards
    him just set right beside him
He just lay his head on my chest
    without saying a word

Got Lost On The Way

Trying to catch the frame she
got caught up in the game
Now everybody knows her
name she's the night time star
On the corner everyday can't
nobody tell her it's a better way
She loves using her body instead of
her brain
The money got her in
Got her started got her thinking
got her changing her ways
It never used to be this way
She was a smart pretty girl
Always thinking of a brighter world
Until she met a guy who change her
whole mind one day
Now there's no turning away
She walks the streets trying to
bring him his dreams
He makes her seems she's in
control of everything

The money the power the frame
gave it in the palm of her hand
So young so young can't you
see it's just a kid living a
false dream
No way out no way out that's what
other people sees
But to her it's the best place to be
She feels that's her best friend her
man her protector
In reality he just another man
who is using her abusing her
dragging her to her grave
But she can't seem to understand
this concept no it won't get
through her head
No, she wants to be blind by the wolf
in lamb clothing that's how she
ends up die

I'm Standing

I'm standing up on this stage
To say what's on my mind
I been getting rape and abused
By my mom boyfriend
That she still lives with until this
  very day
You rape me and took my love away
Made it hard for me to trust a guy
  that loved me
You said I wouldn't make it
You said I wouldn't be nothing in
  life but shit in it
But yet here I stand in front of
  you today
As a senior graduate from college
Yeah, my last year was today
I just wanted to say
Even though you took my
  virginity away
Put myself self-esteem down
I still made it and I forgive you
But not for you
But for me to set myself free
From not being scared to trust or
  to love any other man
After what you did to me
I'm free from any pain you gave me

I Can't Be A Burden

I don't want to go home
Don't want to be a burden
Don't go nothing to tribute
So, what's the point of even going
I'm looking for a way out
Tell me if you see one
Living in a struggle got me fighting
   just to be someone
But if God can hear my cries
   at night
Than one day he'll answer
   my prayers
And life itself can be more alright
Tell me if you can feel my plight
But I'm on a fast lane
I know I'm at risk at losing my life
But if I can put food on my table
   why not
I do what I got to do
So how can you judge me

If you never walk in my
   shoes before
Me making seven dollars and fifty
   cents an hour isn't enough
When the cost of living is
   constantly going up
I know I put myself in harm way
But I didn't care
If it enables me to give my family a
   better life
So, I'm stacking up
Rather you see it or not I'm going
   to make a way
It might not be the best one
But if this is all I know
This is all I been shown
Than where can I go
Tell me do you see a way
Please let me know
Because my clock is ticking

She Walks Alone

She walks alone
She never really had a home
She by herself in the world
that's all she knowns
Her mother died when she ten
After that it all went down hill
from than
She had to become a woman at the
age of ten
She got put in foster care each
home she went to she ran
away from
Only because she was getting
sexually abuse

How she felt like nobody
understood her life or the pain
she was going through
Now she's fourteen years old sailing
her body to grow men she
doesn't even know
How she wanted to stop having sex
each and everyday
But she knew she couldn't because
she wouldn't have a place
to stay
So this is what she do every
single day

He's In The Gang

He's in the gang he still remains
He hanging near the corner
   with his friends
Selling what's in his pockets
Until it's nothing left but dead
   presidents
Everything is like a game
He doesn't care for the love he
   never had
He the type who doesn't care if he
   lives or die
He doesn't have nothing to live for
   in life
Every female he meets he mistreat
Rather your good or bad the same
   rules apply

If you are his old head or
   right-hand man
He looks out more than well
Telling him to check someone off
   the bucket list
He'll do it without even thinking
   twice it's liking rolling dice
He doesn't fear anything for he
   been through too much that he
   could careless
He's sixteen young and reckless
   cold hearted
He used to come to school
But after seven months he stops
   showing up

Don't Tell

Don't tell nobody what I been
doing to you
What goes on behind these
closed doors
Stay between me and you do you
understand me
Be shhhh and quiet and no more
harm will come to you
Hide your abuses when go to school
If the teachers ask questions just
make up some excuse
Don't ever tell them the truth
Go head try to tell your mom

She won't believe you
You know she loves her men more
then she does you
She'll put you right in front of her
Just to save her men from walking
out that door
Be shhhh and quiet when I come
into your room
Be shhhh and quiet when I'm
touching you
Be shhhh and quiet until I'm no
longer there

Life Keep Passing By

Life keep passing me by
No matter how much I try
You want to pause and rewind
When your young you don't think
about life
Until it's too late to think
Always living for today never
for tomorrow
When your grade drop
It doesn't matter to you
Since you think you aren't going to
live to see the day
You graduating from high
school anyway

You use to say how you wanted to
go to college
So you could be a basketball player
Now it's just about getting by
You don't even try to make
it through
Don't care about life like you
used too
It's November now
You don't come to school no more
If you were still here sitting
beside me
I would had kept pushing you on
But your dead and now your gone

She Scared

Looking into her eyes there's fear she scared
I want to hold her
Tell her it's okay
That there is a better way
But she looking down at that
    bridge ready to jump over
I see her I see her clear as day
I'm running towards her please wait
But I can hear her thoughts
What is there to live for
I just lost my only friend
Who was my only sister
Who is now dead and gone
No one to turn to no one to care
    for the little girl
Who only had a little sister to
    live for
I see her tears falling from her eyes

The hurt the pain is marked deep
    under her soul
I yelled again she turns looking
    my way
I can't quite see her face
But she's a young beautiful girl
    with long brown hair blowing
    into the wind
I watch her climb onto the pole of
    the gate till she was standing
    on top of it
By that time, I'm just three seconds
    away from her
She looks my way again saying death
    can take me too right before she
    hop's over
I reach for her and caught her hand
When she looked up, I realize it
    was me

Young Kings

We were young kings
remember just playing
around
Trying to figure out different ways
to escape from this hell
We had our own little plans on how
we were going to make it out
When the time came how we was
going to help out
At the end of the day all we had was
each other
We didn't have a family until we
became brothers
I'm thinking about how you actually
understood me
Who actually took the time to
actually get to know me
We had the same struggles
The same problems
The same stories
I swear nobody knew how I
was feeling
When I find out you got shot
and kill

They say you got into an argument
and things went left field
I couldn't never see you saying
anything too crazy
To the point where you're no longer
living anymore
In the end of the day we were
just kids
Only seventeen and sixteen just
trying to live
Ever snice you past away
I been more ambitious
I drop out of high school just to get
my GED
I went straight to college
I'm still going to make the dreams
we plan come true
I always remember us saying one of
us had too
So, I'm still going to do it just
for you
The only difference is it's me
instead of you

Struggle

What's living in the struggle
Is when you checking
the refrigerator when it's
nothing to eat
Sharing the same bed with five
different people
Don't got much to live for but you
still dreaming
Fighting so much it's like you at war
Hustling just to have a come up
When it never matches up
Someone is always knocking you
Someone is always trying to take
the last thing you got
So you have no choice but to be
a fighter
You got to be a survivor
You got to take care of yours

Nobody who haven't live this
doesn't understand this
This life isn't easy
We carry our struggles on our backs
Some how we still smile
We still glow we still shine
When we make it to the top
Know it wasn't easy
It's a lot of scars you don't see so
don't misjudge
Remember you're standing on the
other side of the grass
So don't forget this
Some things you really don't know
So be very careful when it comes
to judging
Don't be the fool and just assume

Crazy Life

She trying to walk in grow
    woman shoes
    When the shoes barely fit
Trying her best to be older than
    what she really is
Messing with grow men thinking
    that's mature
Hanging with the wrong type
    of friends
Got her miss behaving in school
Mother isn't there
Father was never around
Baby girl is on her own basically
    raising herself
This is the life she was giving
There's no changing it
She's like fuck the world that's
    exactly how it is
Hit up a club one night with a
    couple of her friends
She wasn't even old enough to be
    there yet she still got in

She seen a man that caught
    her eyes
That was looking at her all
    night long
He finally walks up to her
He starting to talk his game to her
Got her smiling got her giggling
Got her a few drinks now she ready
    to leave with him
She said goodbye to her friends
    that she'll contact them later
Hop in his car because that wasn't
    her first time
Took her to a hotel because he had
    a wife and kids at home
Next day he woke up she was
    already gone
While getting wash and dress
He finds something she left
It was a beautiful locket that was
    written mother and daughter
He didn't think nothing of it even
    when he opened it

But if he actually looks at the picture
He would had realized that was his
       under-age daughter

Chapter 2
LOVE GAIN & LOVE LOST

So Many Times

So many times, I try
Some many times, I fell
So many times, I wonder about
   you and I

So many things we did
So many things that we said
So many things that I didn't tell

If only I had another chance
I would turn everything all around

So many times I seen you
So many times I said hi
I should had walk away and said bye

So many times, I ask myself
Did I make a mistake
Between you and I

In this life we would never know
For you're with someone else and
   so am I
I just used to wonder about
   you and I

He Gives

He gives me the strength to go
on about my day
He holds me when I'm feeling
lost or confuse
He kisses me when my soul is
singing the sad blues
He makes love to me when I need
that special refill to rejoice me
Oh, when he smiles
Oh, my gosh when he smiles
My heart would just stop only for
that short movement
He gives me the kind of tenderness
that I never even knew existed
in a world like this
So, when he questions why I
like him
Why I want him
Why he matters to me
I'll simply read him this
He keeps me safe in his heart safely
tuck away

Where's nobody able to touch me
only him
The best part is he's all mine and
I'm all his
I'm just glad I finally found him
or should I say him finally
finding me
But either way he's more than
I need
He's more than I image him to be
This is my king rather he knows he
is one or not
I'll make him feel like one to me
The things he got me feeling
It's not like it just sexually or just
plan lust
No, it's deeper than anything that
lust or sex can instore
He got me feeling like a little girl
with a crush
I just love the feeling he gives
I love the way he got me

And I just can't deny it
Snice it's writing all over me
It's like he already blueprinted on me
    just by the love he gives me alone
That's why you'll see me with this
    smile or glow on me
Yeah, he's the one who put it one me
    and I couldn't thank him enough
    for it

Don't Take

Tell me how many pieces you
need from me
Tell me how much I got to give
to make you whole
I know I'm not the one who
broke you
But you putting me through hell
I'm really trying to figure out what
you want
Tell me what's going on with
you honestly
Tell me what you feeling the most
Tell me if it's someone new who
got you
I know it's not just me
I know I can't be getting lead on
I know everything you said
I know what lays between
your mind
When I walk by feeling the coldness
When we make eye contact and
get wordless

When you feel something but can't
express it
It's more confusing than religion
What's going on we can't even tell
no more
We can't connect
We can't react
I rather leave everything in the past
I rather forget about the love we
once had
I rather let go before I have a
break down
This is no good
This is unhealthy
This is bad for sure
I'll wipe your tears away
Before I'll kiss you goodbye
I'll huge you one more last time
I hope the next stage in life is more
beneficial
I hope it's nothing but progress

Not Herself

She doesn't trust the same
no more
Everything is different her
emotions is not there
She gives herself away
She gives her smiles away
She tries to make other people day
She tries to hide her own pain
Every guy wonders about her
Every guy gets interested when she
walks by
Close off she really is
Distance is her middle name
She could make you laugh
She make you forget about
your sorrow
She brings joy

That energy she gives
That positive vibe everyone wants a
piece of
Love it when she's around
Love it when she speaks her mind
Love it when she got the answer to
the problem
Love it when she's can solve them
No one is there for her
No one actually knows her
What they see is what they believe
She going through her own
personal battles
That she'll never bring to the table
Only God really knows her name
Only God knows her heart and soul

Tell Me

Tell me if this is love or lust
Tell me if you know the
difference between the two
I want to know if your
playing around
I'm trying to figure out what's
going down
I want to know what I'm really
getting myself into
You say you want me but is it true
You say I got you like no one else do
When I come around boy
I can tell the difference boy
I know the feeling I'm getting
No matter what you are saying
Your body language is speaking a
whole different language
Tell me if I'm wrong or right
Tell me if I'm not getting straight
to the point
I don't want to keep going back
and forth
I don't want to keep questing this
like we at war
There's no need to raise your voice
There's no need to try to over
talk me
When you keep your head down low
I can see the truth inside of you
I can tell your just using it as a sad
love song instrumental
When you say you don't know who
to trust
It's not like I was every in a rush
I took my time never once did I put
up a fuss
I just don't plan on being no fool
If you wanted me you would had
show me
If you care for me you would had
been there for me
If it wasn't just me, I should had
been the only one
You were holding in your arms

Tell me what was the point in
    seeing me
Tell me what was the point in talking
    to me
If I couldn't do nothing for you and
    you couldn't see yourself with me
I just want to know
I just want to know why
I know that's a question you'll
    never answer
I know that's the reason why I
    stop caring
That's the reason why you never
    really did quite get me

When I Find Him

I been watching you for a awhile
They say that I'm hopeless
    for love
That I just can't keep my head out
    the clouds
That I still be wishing on the stars
Hoping for someone that's
    really mines
That I might find him some day
We could prove everyone wrong
How love still exists and it still
    remains strong
But I haven't found you yet
So, I just set and think how we
    would be
How I would be there for you
How I wouldn't ever compared you
    to any another man I had
You'll be the only one for me and I'll
    be the only one for you

You can just talk to me telling me
    what's on your mind
I'll be the one you vent too
I'll be the one to ask you how was
    your day
And when you really having
    bad days
And we can't seem to meet eye
    to eye
I remember to try my best letting
    you know this is nothing but
    a test
That every couple goes through
    a rough patch but I still won't
    leave you
Even if we don't meet eye to eye
My heart is forever yours so there
    are no goodbyes

Bad Habits

I'm trying to figure out what I'm
doing wrong
I'm wondering why you don't
pick up no more
Is it something that I said most of
those things I never met
All I think about is you and
how these other guys can't
replace you
But we not doing the same things
that we used too
You had me falling for you
You had me missing you when you
weren't around
I'm trying figure out if you're
playing now
Should I do the same thing
Should I say I'm single now
When all I really want is you
I'm trying to see if you'll
come through
None of these females can be me

So, don't start screeching what you
had in me with someone new
Let me know what you want me
to do
I don't got time for guessing games
I'm just want to know if I'm wasting
my time with you
I'm not feeling the distance
between us
The communication is falling off
Let me know if you're playing house
with another
Let me know if this was all just
a front
I know I'm kind of being all blunt
I just really want to know
I know I should take signs instead
of words
But I need to hear it just for me to
feel it
I'm looking at my phone thinking
about calling you

Even if you don't answer I'm still
     going to say fuck you
Then you'll contact me saying why
     I'm acting like that
You'll say I need to chill there's no
     need to trip relax
Then you'll talk game like you
     always do
Than everything repeats itself like it
     always do

I Loved You

Yeah, I said it I love you
I'm not going to front on you
I know I didn't say it as often
To you as I was supposed to
I figure I didn't have to
If I show you more than I had too
I put years in with you
Tell me who was really messing with
    you the way I do
When you lost your right
Who was there holding you
Who was there consoling you
Was it not I was it not me
Saying don't worry I got you
While wiping your tears away from
    your eyes
Wasn't I even there for you
Even more on those days you had
    nothing to offer me
No matter what type of struggle
    you were in
I made sure I never left you

Instead I chosen to help you
I chose to make things alright again
Everybody said you never did
    deserve me
If they ask me back than
I would say they all wrong
    about you
Because there wasn't nothing
    better than you
Only God came before you
Everything I had I made sure you
    had it too
You were my man
how could you ever dare say I
    wasn't there for you
Did I not spoil you was I not making
    love to you
I did my best to try to uplift you try
    to inspire you
But yet you chose to leave me
    because I wasn't enough
    for you

You told me you wanted more of
what I was giving only with
someone new
I guess you didn't know half of these
fucking females can only do half
of what I do
Shit I was in love with you
I did more than admire you
I did more than appreciate you
How could you dare say I didn't
love you
You must get me confused with
those hoes you were fucking
around with
If you knew all the things, I gave up for
you maybe you would be acting
different
but none of that matters to you
I stayed trying to crown you
I stayed trying to make you my king
But you can't crown no man who
wasn't born to be no king
I had to find that out the hard way
No matter what I say I still can't put
nothing against you

My friends say I'm soft since I chose
to forgive you
But I couldn't hate you
Why put more time and energy in
Then I actually did love you
You got a new girl now
I heard she having a son by you
It's crazy how this all happened
After you broke it off with me
If it turns out to be yours
I'm going to take the time out to say
congratulations to you
I know I probably shouldn't be saying
anything at all to you
I should say fuck you
But I care for you
But I wish the best for you
I hope you truly happy now
I hope she's really the one for you
Now let me focus now
Now let me let this go now
Now let me get right back to making
this money cash flow

Do You Get Me

I love the sound of his voice
I love the base of it when
    he talks
He got me smiling
He doesn't even know the
    reason why
He got my head up in the clouds
God, I got to come back down
    to earth
Before I get lost in his eyes
I promise this won't happen
    every time
He won't stay away he love my vibe
I feel like he been waiting it all
    the time
Distance doesn't last long
Before he starts hitting up my line
He good with his words just like I'm
    good with mine
We getting caught up
We getting rush up
To the point it scared the hell out
    of us

We not really trying to get
    emotional involved
No, we not we got trust issues
    it's more complicated than
    we thought
Second guessing goes past
    our minds
When we together it's a whole
    different level
That's why stay talking all the time
When was the last time you
    connected with a person
    intellectually
It's not even about sex it's
    more mentally
Want to know how you think
Want to see what you see
It's a difference believe me
Some who wants to help build you
    up in all means
How many of ya'll really know what
    I mean

Brand New

How long does it take
For someone start acting
different
Is less than a month or a year
Can it be done that same day
Forgetting that you ever care
That nothing was ever real
Number block you got straight
to voice
Can't use social media you cut
off there
Feelings got involved but you
don't care
Call someone else up you they
going to be there

Until that another person wants
you back
But you curved on them for playing
with you like that
Now they in their feelings because
always thought they can
get back
But now they going to call
someone else
Given the same line they just gave
It doesn't matter as long as it not
you that they coming too
Said the hell with them you been
doing you and nothing better
than focusing on you

Past History

I see your full of trouble
While your eyes are lock on me
You say I'm your type
That I got more than what you like
Keeping my distance is what I
   do best
Avoiding complete conversation
Only saying hi and bye
You're the trouble type and I'm just
   trying to do myself right
I know it all seems so sweet and
   beautiful
I know the attraction is the
   death round
I step more than three steps back
I know your no good
Always hurting everyone you love
Always trying to be controlling
So please excuse me for being
   in the wrong place at the
   wrong time
Just pretend to be blind

Just pretend you never seen me
Just pretend our eyes never made
   eye contact
That I never walk by and you never
   said hi
That you never ask to know
   my name
Trouble guys don't mix well when
   you're trying to do right
I'm not feeling the vibe
I'm not feeling the
   opposite attraction
I'll kiss it long goodbye into
   the night
This is nothing but past history
I know one day you'll change
I know one day you'll be a
   completely different guy
You'll have a whole
   different mindset
But right now, that's neither the
   day or the time

From The Distance

I said I love from a distance
I know you messing with the
same check
That's why I'm not going back
to you
You keep saying you're different
You're not the old you that I
once knew
But I don't trust you to believe it
I been a fool for you more
than twice
Yeah, I was dumb stupid too
But everybody kept saying love
comes with a sacrifice
I know probably won't believe it
But I don't have any more chances
to give to you
So, I'll be moving on now
I'm saying goodbye now to
everything we once knew
Being in love with you wasn't the
best thing to do

I doubted every moment
when you were out caught
messing around
I just kept saying it wasn't true
There's no hiding it or denying it
no more
I won't allow myself to feel sad
over it
The love you had for me wasn't the
same as mines
If it was you would have never did
what you done
Without it being able to hurt you
like it's hurting me right now
Those tears you cry you can just
wipe away from me
All your secrets all your lies finally
came to my eyes
You were living a double life
I guess that's why question was I
cheating most of the time
I should have paid attention to
the signs

But I was completely happy thought
    you were too
I thought I was the only women
    for you
Why ask to get married if I wasn't the
    one for you
Love is completely blind for sure and
    that's the God honest truth
I mean shit who knew

I'm Past The Point

See girls might not get it
But I'm pass he fine as
hell stage
Yeah you might have waves inside
your waves
Your natural curls may out curl
goldilocks any day
That gorgeous smile you got that
brings out your eyes every time
A body that doesn't need to
be redefined
It's more perfect than wine
I can see what you got every time
you put some sweatpants on
When it comes to physical
attraction you know how to
turn it on
But let's step back after I see you
got that
Now I want to know does your
mental match
What you have to offer that I can
actually invest

If all you got is look than you going
have to take that left
I'm going to need your intellectual
to match
Looks may get you through the
door with others
But it only gets you halfway
through the door with me
If you don't have no real quality
than you just not the one
for me
I'm past that stage where looks is
not enough for me
Since I am an investor, I have to see
what type of stocks you have
for me
I'll show you things I have to
offer you
It can be a take it or leave it or see
where it goes kind of thing
But long story short I hope you got
more than looks for me

Do You

He said I'm the type of woman
    he likes
    But am I the type you'll value
I don't like mind games
Can you be true because my style
    is nice
How I carry myself got you wanted
    to take a bite
But before you get hype just know
    my standards can be high
I might over work you just to
    show you
that you can reach the things you
    thought you couldn't do
You will get a chance if you can
    prove you are a good man
I can be your ride or die just know
    everything takes time
So, come to me allow me to explore
    your mind

I want see to how well you can
    represent yourself
No this is not a test
It's more like a pop quiz
I want you to make it to the
    finish line
Come on catch up to these
    green lights
Tell me which way you flowing so
    we can float together
I'm all about building and leveling up
so, give me that drive and I'll feed
    you mines
Let's kiss these hardship goodbye
Let me close your eyes
Let me give you a surprise
Let me show you how well our
    world can intertwine
It's looks so fine just like old wine

Your Choice

Tell me if I'm what you're missing
Tell me if I'm what you've been
looking for
Since a young little boy
Tell me if I'm the woman you had
been dreaming of
You stay confusing me on what you
actually want
You want to hold me
You want me near you
You say you miss me
Then you'll push me away
Then you'll stop communicating
with me
Then you'll say you can't do this
no more
Tell me which one it is
Tell me which mood are you
feeling today
Do you want to be all up
underneath me
Do you want to be kissing all
over me

Saying you want a family
Saying you want a
spiritual connection
Saying you want a long-term
relationship
Saying you want marriage
Don't you know that takes time
Don't you know that takes efforts
Don't you know that comes with
understanding
Not someone who ready to walk
out when things don't go
as plan
If you don't got the patience your
nowhere ready for a long term
Sorry if I had to pop your bubble
Just to let some light in for
this situation
But I couldn't allow you to
walk away
Without you seeing the full details
in this picture

He Got You

He got you pretty well
He got you feeling yourself
He got you up against that wall
Your body is not your own
Every time he touches you
Every time he kisses you
You give your mind and soul
He knows you pretty well
He knows your different
   favorite spots
Where every time you say no
When every time you say you can't
He just makes you say yes
He just makes you say you can
   and will
Every time you open your legs it's
   a gateway
There's no denying him
There's no leaving him
He got you pretty damn well
He got you feeling things that you
   didn't know

there's no running away from
   him now
You say he can be that one
You say can it be this real
He told you what he wanted
He told you he could get it
   from you
If he ever really put his mind to it
He said he was great with words
He said he knew how to get inside
   of your heart and mind
You dare him to take that step
You dare him to cross that line
So, he did without even hesitating
He played it every smart
He laid all his cards down just right
   to get you where you are now
The only damage is you falling
   in love
You can't seem to let him go
You always want more arounds
You always want more than what
   he's willing to give

He would say you knew what it was

He would say you knew exactly what I

    was more willing to offer

I chose you just like you pick me

Don't go asking for more

That's not what we sign up for

I didn't make the rules you did

I told you before don't get upset

    when things don't go how

      you plan

I was never the love man

You knew that before I ever

    approach you

You just thought it would be me and

    not you

And yeah, I hear about you too

I know things that you do

I just wasn't going to get played no

    not by you

Double Standers

The double standards belief
She slept with you the first day
Decided to open up her garden
to you Unbeknownst to you
The time she took debating rather
this was the right thing to do
Even if this was her first time
or not
The fact she felt able to trust you
Without being misjudged
or misused
You made her feel as though
everything was okay
So, when the time came you got
what you wanted
Did a lot to convince her you
weren't a thief in the night only
looking for what he can get
and steal

Now you were on a different page
we can talk we can chill I'm
not really looking for that kind
of thing
So, when she opened up her
garden, she decided to feed you
her fruits
She put all her hard work into
growing these things.
For you to mislead her
For you to call her out of her name
I'll advise you to think twice
Before you say another thing

Love

I never been in love
So, tell me what it was
I just met you only a few days ago
You already running through
    my mind
I know I never been in love
But is it possible this could be the
    first time
When I catch your eyes
It's like a natural high
Caution should be aware
Your unoriginal charm got
    me floating

Your intelligence got me wondering
Hey handsome tell me where you
    came from
Did you came from my left or right
I never saw you actually coming
You got me in a daze
While your smile keeps taking
    me away
I never been in love
I never been in love
Until the day I met you

My Worth

Baby I want to know if I'm
worth the time of day
Am I worth the love and
attention that you might be
giving away
I want to know if I'm worth more
than diamonds and pearls
Am I worth the wait or patience
Am I worth that extra mile to you
I want to know am I worth the
moon and stars that's giving
at night
I want to know am I worth the
loyalty and respect
Am I worthy to show to your family
Am I worth any other women that
you might have your eyes set on
I want to know what I stand as to
you as young women
Do I come as something less or
something more to you
I want to know am I someone
special to you or just a piece of
crap to you

I want to know am I worth telling
your secrets too
Am I worth being real to
Am I worth holding on to
I want to know am I the one that
make you simile
When your world doesn't shine
for you
That calms you when you're having
a rough time or maybe
Am I just someone you're just
playing around with for fun
Am I just someone you're just
fronting for
Only to pretend you have an
interest for
I want to know am I worth to be
cherish by you
I want to know am I worth the
effort to make it last with you
Or is possible that I could only be
just sex to you
Someone you want when you
need her

But when she needs you
You'll walk straight out on her
Than act like y'all never had real
    conversations before
I want to know what is between me
    and you
What's my worth to you
What's my worth to you
I want to know does it mean anything
    to you
What am I worth to you because if
    you can't find it or see it
I don't mind showing you
But if you choose not to pay
    attention to it
 Don't get upset if it happens to walk
    right pass you
I just wanted to know was I ever
    worth anything to you

My Joy

I'm his heart
I'm a part of his soul
I'm one of the reasons why he
  glows
I give him my love to keep him going
I'm one of his inspirations
I'm his number one supporter along
  with our daughter
I stand as his reflection
The way I carry myself
The way I speak

The way I hold my head up
It's because of him
Gave me more than confidence
Gave me more than Knowledge
Gave me more than strength
I know not everyone going to
  understand it
For my man for my loving husband
There's really nothing I can't do
What us together that's living proof

Relatuonship Not Lasting

I'm trying to figure out why
relationship doesn't last forever
Why it's not common no more
You just couldn't solve the problem
Did someone kept lying
Someone being miss treated
Someone out there cheating
Or did the love just fade away
Forgot how to enjoy one another
Forgot how to communicate
Or did someone need space
Or did someone jump in to fast

Rush the whole relationship thing
Or did someone get bored
Someone wanted more
Did someone become insecure
Did someone become unsure
Did ya'll start arguing more
Someone trying to control everything
Started playing games
I'm trying to figure out why it
    doesn't last no more
Tell me what is forever anymore

Don't Stop Believing

I know I have my weak
movements
Temptation is a bitch
I wish I never did what I did
I wish I never made you cry
I never meant to hurt you
So I apologize rather you accept it
    or not
I know I was wrong
I know I should had stayed with you
Loving you was never easy
But I keep pushing anyways
I know you probably hate me
You probably turn into something I
    never wanted you to be
Saying fuck love
It's all about getting money now

When we both know you want more
You airing everything out
I see you're still venting
Got you talking bad about women
Don't get closed off
Don't stop believing because of me
It's good woman out there
Who would do more than me
Who would be better for you
    than me
I'm sorry that I broke your heart
Your love I couldn't handle
I got scared so I folded
Had you standing by yourself
So please forgive because you
    deserve the best
Even if that woman wasn't me

How Hard

How hard can you fight for us
How much can you try for us
Can you take your time
Can you listen
Can you actually love everything
    about us
Even with the good and bad
Can we heal from the past
Can we grow like we tended
I know you love me
You know I love you
So, what are we doing
What's the next move
I'm getting tired of the drama
I want to make love and make up
How can you leave
How can you say goodbye to me
I keep giving you all my energy
I want to rebuild to make
    us stronger
It's me and you only me and you
I just want to be happy with you
Tell me what's wrong

Tell me what should we work on
Because you're my best friend my
    best team mate
Your more than a soul mate
I'm not giving you a false dream
I'm giving you reality
So, keep your eyes open
Can you see the beauty in us
Can you see the
    unconventional love
Can you see the miscommunication
    that happens sometimes
How people can hate what we have
Try to ruin what we got
We can't listen to the hearsay when
    it's never proven
Don't compare us to other people
    relationships
Don't misjudge us
That's how we fall off
That's how the war begins
Now we out talking each other
No one is listening

Let's put out the flames

I don't like how the fires grows

Let's calm down

Let's relax let's rethink

Now tell me what's wrong

Can you take your time

Can we both listening and

    comprehend what we are saying

Can we see both sides of the story

Don't quite and move on when things

    get to hard

I just want to grow and move on

Genuine

Tell me if I'm everything you
need in a woman
Tell me if I'm everything you
wanted and more
Tell me if you believe I'm the only
one that's right for you
That God created me hand made
just for you
That I'm where your heart belongs
That I'm more than your home
When you missing me, you'll do
anything just to see me
Call me just to hear me say
your name
Talking to you night and day when
your far away
When we see each other again it's
nothing but hugs and kisses
Asking what should we do today
Have a movie night
Have a game night
Or just stay home cuddling and
play fighting

It's no need for me to be with
someone else besides you
I know for sure your more than
my joy
The connection we got is better
than two best friends
We can argue we can disagree
and still find have peace in
each other
When another beautiful woman got
her eyes on you
I don't stress it at all when your
eyes always lock on me
When I'm gone you constantly
looking for me
When you gone, I'm constantly
asking for you
Even when we never that far from
each other
I don't know why we feel this way
I don't know why we act this way
You give me everything I
always need

You make sure I'm on top of my game
You make sure I never give up on
    my dreams
You even help me bring some of them
    to reality
Our love is beyond strong all the
    things we been through as a
    couple and we still stand strong
I know sometimes we both can be
    complicated
Not wanting to talk on what's
    really wrong
Since we learn how to work with each
    problem
we got better at solving them
We're perfectly imperfect together
Even if we don't match, we still work
There's no need to complain when
    we're both genuinely happy

Chapter 3
TRAP

Alone

I feel alone nobody is trying to
move along
They just sit there and just do
as they told even though they
question it
They won't ever raise up angst it I
see it for what is it
Fear in our souls that they blue
printed there for control
Can we break this chain can we be
set free or would we stay blind
Since where to scared to face the
harsh reality of this time
We all try it at least once some of
us make it and some of us don't
If we continue to take this same
route there won't be no hope
Our history would be covered in lies
with blood laid upon it

Think, think, think for yourselves
think for your family or
Friends what's best for them for
this whole country because
If we don't the next thing you know
we all end up on the same floor
The rich the middle class and the
poor at the bottom
Where nobody shines just darkness
only in the spot lime
I want to change this world but I
can't do it alone
I need my great speakers I need my
great leaders we can't be quite
no more
This is now war for our gradation
least take control
Starting today were saying no more

Keep Your Head Up

I want to know how you been
I want to know what's been on
   your mind
What you got being so distance and
   towards yourself
What you going through that you
   feel as though you can't let
   me know
Don't you know I can see your pain
   no matter how hard you try to
   hide it from
Don't you know I'm here if you
   need me
Don't you know I can wipe away
   your tears
Even when I'm not there
My words are still able to heal
That I do have a good listening ear
That I can make you laugh out loud
   even when your soul is crying
I can solve some of your problems

I can make you see things
   differently to show you that
   your never really standing alone
That your quietness speaks louder
   than words
That you can do way more than
   what you think you can
That your worth way more than
   what you think you are
I'm not trying to gasp you up I just
   what to get you thinking more
Maybe no one ever push you that far
Maybe no one never really
   challenge you in that
   way before
To let you see the best thing
   you can do is be competitive
   between yourself
To really see the different on how
   much you actually grew from
   the things you went through

Cause no one understand your pain
or reasons why better than you
and God
And nothing wrong with getting help
sometimes because once in a
while we all need
Don't let your pride get in your way
from what you're thinking
Don't let it get in the way from
asking what you truly want to say
Sometimes people come into your
life just to help you keep your
up head
And sometimes they don't sometime
they want to make you miserable
as they are
But for the ones that really do right
by you just hold closet because
those are the ones that's hard to
come by
I know you probably heard this
all before

And what I'm speaking is nothing new
Don't go getting anger when people
walk in and out your life
Just take what you can learn from it
and move on from it
Even if it might come hard at
movements
Cause everything can be a lesson and
a blessing at the same time
If I was able to show you a different
world that's way better than this
I wouldn't mind taking you to
it myself
but I'm still trying to figure out
where's that place at for myself
If we ever happen to fall off or not
talk anymore
I hope this be one of my poems that
you'll always remember me by
the most

None The Less

I was told not to cry
When I'm going through hard times
I was told to push through
   while smiling
Turn a dove into a bean
Flipping money isn't easy
I grind for mines nonstop
If you want it
Best believe you'll bleed for it
I don't take losses
I just reelevate
My parents taught me well
I know when to hold back now
I know when to let lose
I know how to check anyone
   without their feelings
   being abused
You don't got to fear me
But I won't ever allow you to
   disrespect me
How I move most people can't keep
   up with me

That's why I tell people do your
   own thing
Everything isn't for everybody and
   that's the reality
I'm learning while I'm going through
   my own testimonies
So, if I act up
If I show off
It's because I'm actually finally
   feeling it now
I know life isn't easy
It's a difference when you
   had nothing
But somehow still made a way to
   bring a meal to the table
That's another level of
   achievement
So, I know how to hustle
So, I don't live in sorrows
Not everyone can feel this
Not everyone can relate to this
But if you are a hustler, you'll
   understand this

The Game

I'm fighting a war that's already been won
I'm giving and trying but I'm already in
I'm counting down the past
I'm counting down how old I am
I can't control anything I'm just reliving everything
I see the same people all over again
We question how many times we met like this
I know it's something that I just can't explain

But once I remember I'll be replaced again
It's a game I'm a part of that I can't win in
The rules are always changing
The game gets harder each time I think I know what's going on
Everything shakes than it breaks than rebuild itself in different forms again
I know I'm a threat the game itself has a target mark on me
Only a few will ever see this

I Want Out

If I told all my problems
Do you think you can solve them
I got issues with a lot of pain
I'm trying to be positive
I'm trying to be Inspirational
When I'm living in the gutter
No one actually cares what's goes
    on around here
People life get taken away at a
    young age around here
When you go missing
No one is there looking for you
It's too many of us
so, who care if a few of us
    disappear out of thin air
I'm from the bottom of the bottom
Believe me there is no worst
I don't know how deeper can I go
I don't want to talk about
    my struggles

I just want a way out
That's the only reason why I
    came here
I been told you was the one to help
Honestly, I never believe in you
I never thought you was real
I never seen you
Until that day I hear you said
    my name
I know you are the father of
    all fathers
You're my God
I never knew how lost I really was
    until you call me
I been waiting for so long
It's about time I can finally see
    the sign

Life

Letting go is something we all learn
Growing up is a choice that we can't choose
Having nothing or having something it's up to else
We can give or we can take
We can rule the whole world or we can let life be
Rather we're here or not it will always remain
The earth isn't going no where
Meanwhile we're dying every day
It's a cycle that the living has
It's a lot of things that man will never understand
Until we are actually passed on and gone away
Right now, it's nothing but confusion

Nothing but lies nothing but wars going on
The peace the freedom the joy
We think we know what that is
Until you actually feel that spiritually
Than you see its different levels to each one
Freedom there's nothing weighting on you
Peace there's no worries no fears
Joy there's no depression no sadness here
You know what it means to be living without death being able to touch you
But yet we can't completely describe this in a sensible way

Tell Why Pain Living

Tell me why your standing alone
Tell me why your pushing
everyone away
Tell me why your crying
Tell me what's wrong
Tell me what's really on your mind
Why you don't smile no more
Why you don't date no more
Why you don't love no more
Why you don't try no more
Why is something I need to know
Pain comes and goes don't
you know

Pain isn't a forever thing
Pain can lead to a lot of things if
you keep holding on
Pain shouldn't be the last thing
that remains
Living on is something you
should do
Living for you might bring a change
Living for now not the day before
Living for something new because
the old is old news

I See A Different

It's a war going on
How many of us can tell
We fighting over different areas
  of the city
Some parts we can't cross
Some parts are getting buy out for
  a higher cost
I see separation you can tell
  the difference between an
  upcoming neighborhood
When people with more wealth
  start coming in
They make the schools better
That was once an
  improperly community
After a while you'll see the people
  who originally lived there
  moving out

Only because they can't afford
  their own house anymore
Since their neighborhood value
  went up
What I'm speaking in facts
You'll see it happening right around
  Temple University College
Were they try to buy more
  people house's
You'll see how the
  neighborhood change
It's not all bad but it's not all good
It's a lot of Gender vacation going
  and I don't know how many
  people understood

Already Born With A Disadvantage

Rather I have a child that's
light skin or dark skin
   They would still be treated
the same
Being look as less than a
   human bean
No matter the knowledge I may
   give them
The wisdom I put on them
They could still be look as Ignorant
Even if they're smarter than
   everyone in the class room
See color makes a different like
   beauty does for someone who
   never had it
I see a lot of things and a lot of it
   I question

Racism and discrimination still exist
Those who chose to be blind to it
   are those who can't handle the
   reality for what it is
How black people is label as
Just open your eyes to find out
If you were to watch the news what
   would you see
Would it be a bunch of negativities
   on what is going on in a black
   community
I can see the sign it's not a black on
   black crime
We're just divided it's been that
   way since slavery so more
   than 400 years since it's still
   happening daily

My Father

See my father told me at a
young age
How I was a young Queen
That my beauty might strike some
How my Knowledge and wisdom
could Intimidate
That the color of my skin is hated
Without understanding the full
reason why
This is what I knew
I saw this most of the time

My father try to teach me how my
life would be different
Some people just hate you
even when you didn't do
nothing wrong
My Father told me at a young age
How I was a young Queen
How I was going have to work
harder than some
That I had to be better just to
over come

Old Soul

Would you believe me
If I told you I been here
before
I'm not saying once or twice
I can't remember how many times I die
Or how many times God sent me
back to this earth
I 'am an old soul you know
You can tell sometimes
On the wisdom I give beyond
my youth
I know a lot of things somethings I
just forget
It's like a process that it has
After being reborn some
many times
It's like a mark that never goes a way

I'm old soul living in a young age
I been here before
Would you believe me
If I told you my real age
I seen mostly everything just in
different ways
History has a habit of repeating
itself with me
So therefore, it wouldn't be a risk
If I say I'll see you again someday
In a different century in a
different age
I been here before
Tell God don't send me back
no more
Tell me can you guess my age

God Cry

When it's pouring down
raining outside
You can see God eyes full
of tears
That's the only time God cries
That people actually get to see
But don't realize it's there
When God is hurt

You can feel the pain
Only when it rains
When the lighting comes
It's like a broken smile
That's high in the sky
When you hear the thunder
You can hear the pain
If you ever listen to the rain

Black Men

I love my black men for
many reasons
I could never say their worthless
I could never say they don't make
great father fingers
That they're not one of the
best leaders
That they're not one of the best
educators across the history
of man
I love my black men for
many reasons

How they just can't be so
easily defeated
How they overcome many of their
worst trials
Despite their setbacks that
are giving
Despite the laws that set up
against them
They still tend to strive everyday
They still stand strong in everyway
I love my black men for many
reasons plus more

Broken Queens

If I ever catch a broken Queen
Yeah, I see her soul
My main goal would to be to let
    her shine by giving mines
By showing her, she is still strong
No matter what people think of her
She's better than rubies and gold
Her wisdom is worth more than
    her clothes
Since we all have bad days
    sometimes
I'm here to help on whatever I have
    to fix
I always have my tools with me
No matter what life throws
You may forget this
You may not even remember me
    after this
I stay doing a pretty good job on
    letting what's needed to be known

when comes to fixing
    broken Queens
whenever your tried
Whenever you can't fight your
    battle no more
I come in play I set everything
    in place
I know where everything belongs
    before you even tell me
Don't worry you can finally
    rest take your break it's
    well deserves
Whatever you weren't able to finish
I'll complete it for you
When your back on track more than
    ready to rule
I'll gladly walk back to my thrown

I Hope

You can give your all
    They still watch you fall
    You can give your last
They still won't probably
    appreciate it
You can show them
    unconditional love
They still might toss it in the trash
Not everyone is worth your time
Not everyone is worth that
    helping hand

Can't keep giving every last part
    of you
Can't do it without losing that
    same energy you give
Don't get worn out by people
    out here
Don't get caught up
I hope you really be safe in
    this world

I See

I see the curiosity in your eyes
I see the excitement on your face
I see the potential that stands
   in you
I see the innocents that life didn't
   take away
I see the child in you still plays
Your pretty calm like this
   summer breeze
Your pretty wise for your age
Your beauty grows within time
Your light is something only a
   select few can see

Some people envy you
Some people really try to
   destroy you
But it's something on you that
   shatters you
I see that spiritual shield on you
If you didn't know I'll be the one
   telling you
Someone really protecting you
I just can't see who

To The Man Who Made Who It

I told him to never stop
grinding even when you're fully
successful in it
Always keep hustling so the money
never stops coming in
Now he stacking up his paper until
his safe can't take it
Watching out for those takers
knowing he was one of them
But all that change when he started
focusing on himself
Not listening to the negativity
He shining and blinding everybody
who try to barry him
To the top he goes
Ask him how he feels
He'll said more than good he's
feeling great
Family not starving
No more living in property
Got good credit I'm longer in debt
He's always watching out for
people who be trying to get him

Those females who be wanting him
to slip up
Making it out was all just a dream
Now since it's his reality there's no
going back
To the nightmares he was living
Who said hard work doesn't
pays off
Can't tell him about pain
Can't tell him about losses
Best believe he been through it all
He had that desire
He had that fire
So, when he came up it wasn't
that surprising
But now everyone wants to be
around him
Don't got time for the liars
He only breaking bread with those
who he was struggling with
Not everyone is welcome to his new
life that he created
Some people going to hate it but it
doesn't matter

How Making It Out Started

Hood men is what she like
Since her daddy was of them
Always carry his pipe
His was on the counter every
    other night
Trying to get that money right
Trying to get his family out the
    ghetto just so his kids can have
    a better life
No doubt about it he was hustler all
    the way
But got caught up one day when
    policemen came and got him
He went down with the charges
All he was thinking about who was
    going to raise his son

Teach him how to be a man better
    than he can and it was no one
A pusher man he stops being
Told his baby mom she was going to
    finish college
Because one of them got to
    be successful
If it wasn't going to be him
he was going to make sure it was
    going to be her
Now he's only working to help his
    baby mom through school
Who eventually became his wife
She graduated on the freshmen
    year of their oldest daughter
    going to college

No Negativity

Don't let the Negativity hold
you down
Keep your head up baby boy
There's always a reason to smile
Things can always be worst
And things can always be harder
I know there's a lot pain that's
giving around
But don't you condone it don't you
receive it
Everything can work out for
different reasons
The depression you're in has its
own season
When you have set backs
That doesn't mean it's all over

Nine out of ten you can
overcome that
All depending on where your head
is at
What I'm trying to give you is
motivation
I don't want you to feel
hopeless inside
I came here to break that
I came here to unchain you
I came here to open your eyes
I want you to see that you can
make it
I want to see you living not
just alive

I'm Not Suppose Too

Can you see these chains on me
One on my neck two on my
feet and hands
I'm not allowed to move
I'm not allowed to grow
I'm supposed to be ignorant
Unwise uneducated
Than I'm supposed to pass this on
to my sons and daughters
I'm supposed to have fear instead
of Courage
I'm not allowed to be outspoken
I'm supposed to sit here and
be quit
I was told I couldn't protect
my husband
I was told I couldn't be able to
covers his wounds and scars
I was told I wouldn't be able to
heal him
That I wouldn't be able to help him
When his cuts are bleeding as deep
as mines

I'm not allowed to dream
I'm not allowed to have hope
No, I can't see the bigger picture
I got to be hopeless left in despair
I'm supposed to be look down on
not cherish
It's forbidden it's like a sin
Can't Recognize my beauty
Can't recognize my strengths
Can't recognize my intelligence
That's a whole another interaction
involving disgrace
I'm unwanted women who can't
be love
This train of thought is supposed
to outlast me
Even after my death even after
my time
That's the only thing that's
supposed to grow and carry on
It was programed before me
Before my mother and her mother
before her

But I'll be damn if this is me

So, I started changing history

As you can see, I broke those fucking

    chains off me

Sister

This is my sister
Even though we are not the
same color
She was taught she was better
Since the color of her skin is white
and not blackish
White America said it made a
difference
But yet this is still my sister
My blood streams run in hers
She was taught to hate me, even
though I love her everyday
She was told not to conversate
with me
If it was to speak to me it would
only be to remind me my place

This is my sister that I cater to
That was taken from me
I help her everyday made her life a
lot easier in many ways
My sister who denies me
My sister who forgot me
I'm still apart of you in every way
White America can't white
that away
It's in our DNA can trace it back
to how you are my sister all
over again
But that's another story for
another day I still love you
anyway